30 days of noticing

a simple practice

for greater presence

Copyright © 2021 Alana Sheeren
Published by SheerenVision, Inc.

All rights reserved.
No part of this book may be reproduced in any form or by any means, electronic or mechanical, or by any other technologies now known or later developed, except for brief quotations in reviews, without prior written permission from the author.

For permission write to:
2419 E. Harbor Blvd., #164, Ventura, CA 93001

The resources in this book are provided for informational purposes only and should not be used to replace the expertise of a health care or mental health care professional. Neither the author nor the publisher can be held responsible for the use of the information provided within this book.

Cover and book design by Jenn Cole Design
Cover image by Annie Sprat on Unsplash
Back cover image by Fallon Michael on Unsplash
Author photo by Kristina Donahue

ISBN: 979-8-9853610-0-1

Printed in the United States of America

*For Steve and Ada.
I want to be present
for every moment with you.*

And for Benjamin.

why noticing?

In 2010 my life changed forever with the stillbirth of my son Benjamin, days before my daughter Ada's third birthday. The deep spiral of grief, while parenting a toddler, had me searching for ways to be more present and to live more on purpose. I had spent a lifetime being pulled between following my heart and dreams and trying to please other people. Since those conflicting desires didn't play well together, I spent more time feeling like I was letting everyone down, including myself. I vowed when he died that I would allow myself to feel everything fully and live based on my own truth, prioritizing my needs and not what I thought others needed of me. And for that first year I did.

I wrote a daily blog and was fully present with my emotions. Over time, the grief became less intensely present, and life felt more and more full — a growing toddler, trying to build a business, a husband who was always on the road. By the end of 2012 I was feeling ragged and the self-care I'd put in place after Ben's death had all but disappeared. I wanted a simple, daily way to come back to the moment. I appreciated the way blogging every day that first year of intense loss made me feel more present as I moved through my day. I wanted to remember all the moments that are a part of grief; the daily ups and downs of living with a broken heart; the subtleties of forgetting and remembering; the work of navigating the way my world stopped when it seemed everyone else's kept turning. I don't remember exactly how it came to me — likely in a moment of insight in the shower or while staring at the ocean — but I decided to spend the year writing a daily Facebook post on noticing.

Noticing helped me slow down and pay attention to my senses, to my world, to what was happening around and inside of me. We can notice with or without judgment. It can be a practice to just be with what we notice — our thoughts, feelings and experiences. Noticing is a way to step back from the brink of fear and anxiety, to slow spiraling thoughts, and to interrupt the stories we tell ourselves that may not be true. For example, the 5-4-3-2-1 coping/mindfulness/grounding technique for anxiety is a highly effective and widely used noticing practice: 5 things you can see, 4 things you can feel or touch, 3 things you can hear, 2 things you can smell, 1 thing you can taste.

There is something about writing things down that helps us be more present too. Knowing at the end of the day I was going to share what I noticed meant I was paying more attention as

I went along. Many days, I would sit down to write my post online, think back through my day, and be surprised by what I remembered, by what stuck with me. Over time, I found that I was taking in the world around me in a deeper way — letting it sink in and affect me rather than rushing by. Some days, I was aware in the moment that I was noticing something I wanted to write about. I was noticing myself noticing.

Even as I type these words, I find myself looking at my desk differently. I see the clutter in one area, the stacks of journals with dog eared pages and post-it notes marking places I want to remember and return to again and again. I notice with fresh eyes the pictures and postcards that are stuck to the magnet boards in front of me and they make me smile. I find myself breathing deeper and letting my shoulders slide away from my ears. I'm also noticing a pile I've been meaning to sort for the last two weeks but I'm keeping the judgment out of it. I'll get to it when I get to it. For now, I just want to take in what's here, what's right in front of me, the beauty and the mess, the love and the disaster. It's a practice to hold that space where our full experience is allowed. (My dear friend Liz Lamoreux calls this, "The And Space," which I think is brilliant.) The good news is that with time and awareness, we stretch those muscles and get better and better at being present, with kindness and compassion for our own humanity.

Noticing is a simple way to be present in this moment right now and give yourself the chance to shift the energy of your day (if you want to). It can fill your heart and help you feel connected to a bigger picture, for your own life or for the world.

SPECIAL NOTE
This is not a gratitude practice. It can be — if you choose to be grateful for what you're noticing — but it doesn't have to be. It can be completely neutral and judgment free, or it might make you angry or sad or self-reflective or delighted. Do your best to let it be whatever it is and notice what shows up in the moment.

You can decide to do something with that information. For example: I'm so angry! I need to put on music and let off steam or call my senators or write to my city council or donate to this cause or cry.

Alternately, you can treat this more like a meditation practice as you notice what comes up and let it float away. For example: That made me so angry. I'm going to choose to not engage in that anger right now, but I see how important it is and will come back to it another time.

how to use this book

Take a few deep breaths. Move your body in a way that feels comfortable and good. Wake up your senses. Pay attention to your world a little differently as you go about your day — both your inner and outer world. Choose if you want to carry your book with you, so you can record what you notice as it happens, or whether you want to keep it on your nightstand to reflect on the day before you go to bed at night.

The pages have been left blank intentionally, so you make it YOUR practice. You can write a sentence or a story, a poem or haiku. You can scatter unrelated words over the page or sketch, collage or draw. You can print a photo from your phone and paste it in. It's up to you. All you have to do is open your eyes, your mind, your heart, and notice.

I recommend doing your best to make this a daily practice for 30 days but oh my goodness, please don't use missing a day or two or even seven as a reason to be unkind to yourself. If you don't manage 30 consecutive days, that's perfectly fine. Even one day a week for 30 weeks is better than nothing. I find setting a daily reminder on my phone is a helpful way to drop into presence until it becomes a habit. Find what works for you.

I'll say the same thing about noticing that I say about grief — you are the expert (or you will be) on your own process. Sure, there are guidelines and helpful tips, tools and practices but you're the one who gets to figure out what works best for you. Take these 30 days to explore, to play, to learn about your own needs and desires when it comes to being more present.

And while noticing is a very personal practice, it can help to have company. You might want to find a friend or loved one to practice with. You could share your noticing publicly if you like, on social media or a blog or just in an email to a small group of kindred folks. You could make it a family bonding activity and have everyone in your household contribute at dinner every night.

Make this your own. Make it fun. Make it something you look forward to in your day. Invite the magic of presence into your life — you never know what might change.

Throughout this book, I've included some of the original posts from my Year of Noticing. Use them as ground to push off from for your own daily entries. Yours can be similar or completely different. You can focus on one area at a time (for example, your physical body, the physical world around you, your emotions, your thoughts), although I would challenge you not to put too many parameters around this. Allow whatever wants to be seen (or heard or felt) to arise. You don't have to limit yourself. You can capture one noticing a day or three or ten. Just remember, more isn't necessarily better. Being present to life is the goal.

Are you ready to begin?

Take another deep breath.

And remember: Stay curious. Be kind. Have fun.

today I noticed...

...the way the sky crept from deep turquoise, to indigo, to inky black as the moon inched her way past the palm trees and into my heart.

...that I laughed until I cried twice (and how good that felt). I noticed the extreme close-up mirror in my mother-in-law's bathroom is both amazing and terrifying. I noticed that I continue to fall more and more in love with my daughter.

... gratitude, awkwardness, a twinge of envy, delight, joy and beauty everywhere.

...that I have a tendency not to do "sporty" things because I've had this story my whole life that I'm not good at them. The story goes that I'm only good at dancing/artistic/creative stuff. But you know what? I'm pretty good with a bat and ball. There may be a softball team in my future.

today I noticed...

today I noticed...

today I noticed...

today I noticed...

today I noticed...

today I noticed...

...that tears are always close to the surface with me. They are my response to love, to connection, to truth, to relief and to joy as well as to sadness.

...how odd it is to feel invisible in certain people's presence. I wonder if I make anyone feel that way. I hope not.

...that Ada pronounces observe, "eggzerb" and I want to remember that forever.

...I was afraid of being both too much and not enough. I'm loving and forgiving myself as I feel those old wounds.

today I noticed...

today I noticed...

today I noticed...

today I noticed...

today I noticed...

today I noticed...

...yellow poppies against gray skies. I noticed that hibiscus always makes me think of Benjamin. I noticed that I was in the right place at the right time.

...how loud the wind was when I faced the waves. I noticed the warmth of the sun on my skin. I noticed the way grains of sand shifted suddenly at my feet. I noticed a softening inside.

...how hard I wanted to laugh when my 6-year-old said, "Mama, you sound like you're beside yourself again." And I thought I was handling things well.

...that I'm feeling resentful. It's time to re-prioritize and firm up those boundaries.

today I noticed...

today I noticed...

today I noticed...

today I noticed...

today I noticed...

today I noticed...

...how warmth — whether from the company of friends or the right pair of boots — makes the "I don't feel so good" days easier.

...that nothing went as planned and everything was slightly off. I kept dropping things, bumping into things, I ran the car off a curb trying to be nice and got whacked in the face accidentally by a kid in Ada's music class. At least I'm chuckling about it and feeling grateful these days don't happen often.

...the buzz I get from an idea that sends tingles up and down my spine. I think I'm an idea addict. I'm learning to slow down and breathe into them, seeing which ones stay tingly and which fall away.

...how tears and laughter came at the same moment. Grief and joy. Pain and delight. Side by side.

today I noticed...

today I noticed...

today I noticed...

today I noticed...

today I noticed...

today I noticed...

...the tightening in my chest, the urge to snap at everyone, the frustration, the despair and the doubt that signal an anniversary is around the corner. Monday will be 3 years from Benjamin's stillbirth. (Mama loves you, Ben.)

...how good it was to sit with an old friend. There is nothing quite like shared history to cross the chasm of years.

...heavy eyelids. Purring cat. Anticipation.

...that when I take large leaps, shame often rears up in attempt to keep me safe and small. I noticed what a powerful and painful teacher shame is. I also noticed that my awareness around it has changed dramatically, and I can step outside the experience and observe while still being fully immersed in the feeling. I noticed the moment today's shame went away, and I felt free.

today I noticed...

today I noticed...

today I noticed...

today I noticed...

today I noticed...

today I noticed...

...I felt amazingly at peace during three or four different events that in the past would have triggered big mental and emotional reactions.

...that those 50 yards to the beach can seem impossible to traverse some days, even when everything in my being is saying, "Go look at the ocean." It's interesting to notice when I resist and when I listen.

...what a lovely afternoon I had when I refused to feel guilty about any of the choices I made.

...that frustration is one of my go-to emotional reactions. I'm ready to change that.

today I noticed...

today I noticed...

today I noticed...

today I noticed...

today I noticed...

you did it!

Take a moment to honor yourself for making the effort to be more present to your life. It doesn't matter if you did it exactly the way you wanted to or thought you would. It doesn't matter if you missed a few days here and there or if it took you six months to fill these thirty pages. Choosing to do something different, choosing to break out of a busy routine, even for just a moment a day, is worth celebrating.

If you like this practice and want to take it further, I urge you to do so. Get a small journal you like, or one of those three- or five-year, line-a-day journals. Make it a habit. There are so many gifts in it. A noticing practice not only encourages and supports your being present to your life, it helps you become more self-aware. Reading over your entries, you'll begin to see repetitions and patterns that will point to your values, your deepest desires, your challenges, and your wounds.

Looking back at my Year of Noticing all of these years later, I can see where I've grown, what changes I can celebrate and where I'm still navigating some of the same struggles. While that could be disheartening, it helps me see these places I struggle are baked into my way of being and if I really want to change them, I need to make a concerted effort. I might need outside help — a coach, or a therapist. I might decide to hold these challenges up against different lenses and ask how they fit into my Myers-Briggs type or my Enneagram number, or my astrological birth chart. I can try reframing how I think about them and accepting them as quirks I can learn to live with (and maybe even love). I can wonder if there is a way to turn them into strengths.

A noticing practice reminds us to approach life with a sense of curiosity and kindness. We learn to engage with the world with an open heart and mind, waiting to see what asks for our attention. For example, today as I listened to the radio, I was struck by the contrast in two stories I heard. One was about politicians so deeply entrenched in their partisanship and hunger for power, they were literally allowing their country to run out of fuel and their people to starve. The next told of dedicated humans tromping through wilderness areas in search of endangered plants so they can harvest their seeds and hopefully, one day, plant them in new places to help the species survive. While each story moved me to feel different emotions, I stayed curious, wondering what it is in us humans that can make one person willing to harm and another passionate about helping. Curiosity leads us to learning, to discovery and self-discovery, to new passions and new ways of making the world a better place.

What will you do and who will you be if you allow yourself to keep noticing? Where will this magical journey called life take you, if you continue to practice being present to as many moments as you can?

Wherever it leads you, I hope you remember to breathe deeply, stay curious, be kind and have fun.

With love,
Alana

To Trena Pitchford, for planting the seed for this little book many, many years ago.

To Jenn Cole for your friendship and your beautiful design work. You brought my dream to life, and I am beyond grateful.

To Liz Lamoreux and Lori Portka, for your constant friendship, support and encouragement over the last decade. Thank you for listening to my ideas without judgment and helping me see myself more clearly.

To the Davis & Dawson families — Alexis, Tom, Lauri, Jim, Susan (and Bill), Carter, River and Avalon — for walking beside us in those hardest of days and in the years since.

To my parents, Sarah Jane and John, for your unwavering love and support, and for always believing in me, even if you didn't understand what I was doing.

To Ada, for choosing me to be your mom and for teaching me how big love can be. I wavoo.

To my husband, Steve, for everything.

To everyone who has supported my work over the years, from the blog to the retreats, the podcast and the current documentary project. Thank you for your kind words, your encouragement, your care. It all mattered. It all made a difference to me. It still does.

www.ingramcontent.com/pod-product-compliance
Lightning Source LLC
Chambersburg PA
CBHW060849050426
42453CB00008B/913